Empath:
Survival Guide for Highly Sensitive People

*Overcome Your Fears and Heal
Yourself and Others*

acknowledge that the author is not engaging in the rendering of legal, financial, medical or professional advice. The content within this book has been derived from various sources. Please consult a licensed professional before attempting any techniques outlined in this book.

By reading this document, the reader agrees that under no circumstances is the author responsible for any losses, direct or indirect, which are incurred as a result of the use of information contained within this document, including, but not limited to, — errors, omissions, or inaccuracies.

Table of Contents

Introduction...7

Chapter 1. What Is an Empath, and Are You One?..9

Chapter 2. Being a Highly Sensitive Person in Today's Society...16

Chapter 3. How to Stop Emotional Overload 23

Chapter 4. How to Cope with Anxiety in Big Crowds 31

So What's Anxiety and How Does That Manifest for Highly Sensitive People? 32

Chapter 5. How to Cope with Hypersensitivity on a Spiritual Level....................................38

Initial Disappointment.......................................40

A Lack of Patience 41

A Messy Environment..41

Unhealthy Diet...42

Overthinking...43

Chapter 6. How to Channel Your Emotions and Hypersensitivity into Healing Yourself..................46

How to Emotionally Heal Yourself 48

Biochemistry and Emotional Healing.................52

Emotional Release 55

The Bright Side of Emotional Wounds 58

Chapter 7. Healing Others While Protecting
Your Energy 59

Write Down Your Emotions 60

Meditate 60

Kundalini Yoga 61

Don't Collect Foreign Energies 61

Unplug from the Emotional Fountain 62

Avoiding Malevolent Energies 63

Have Time for Yourself 64

An Emotional Vacuum Cleaner 65

Keeping Your Shield Up 66

Crystals 67

Water Cleansing 69

Nature, the Ultimate "Grounder" 70

Chapter 8. Simple Everyday Habits to Practice
for Feeling Better 72

Having a Morning Routine 73

Setting Daily Goals for Yourself 74

Learning How to Say No 75

Maintaining a Healthy Sleeping Schedule 76

Play around with Creative Activities 77

Get into the Tea Business 78

Balance Your Diet and Consider Exercising.......79

Limit Your Social Media Access..........................80

Surround Yourself with the Right Kind of
People..81

Keep Your Environments Tidy............................82

Add Some Spice to Your Bathing Time..............82

Get Accustomed to Taking Breaks 83

Conclusion..85

How Can They Adjust? 86

Introduction

Being an empath in today's society is no easy feat. If we were to be true to ourselves, we'd realize that even relatively nonsensible people have it rough. There's simply no way to function normally, emotionally speaking, when stress is always there to smack us on the cheek and remind us of all that we could or should be doing and all the versions of ourselves that we could be.

But there is no mistake that people who have an uncanny sensitivity, have it way harder than it should. They feel the pressure of society as a deep visceral feeling that can't be oppressed, and all the problems of the world somehow seem to become theirs. Getting hurt emotionally is an everyday fear, simply because anything can and will cause their hearts to ache. Why? For the reason that their heart is "reachable." The misfortunes of others, the bad mental state of a dear one or just the general "ugliness" of the human nature can easily touch the soul of a sensitive person since there is no protective barrier to keep it away.

That's what this book is about: giving empaths a way

to construct such a barrier—a method of coping with everyday life in a healthy manner, a means of healing yourself and the ones that you reach out to.

Keep in mind that being an overly sensitive person is not a curse. It could be a blessing in disguise. Our world desperately needs this kind of people, those who are in tune with the melody of the universe—those who care just for the sake of caring. So don't take this book as a path to correct some anomaly. It is but a guide to help empaths save others without losing themselves on the way—a gentle push toward better understanding their special abilities and learning to control them rather than letting them dictate their lives.

Be proud of who you are, and get ready to know yourself better, and get a taste of a new kind of happiness: the joy of being you.

Chapter 1. What Is an Empath, and Are You One?

From a psychological point of view, it is widely accepted that an empath is a highly sensitive person with an exceptional emphatic capacity. In other words, they find it easy to place themselves in someone else's shoes and have a deep understanding of their feelings. However, being an empath is not limited to that. It's also defined as having an uncanny intuition, going as far as simply sensing other people's state of mind by only being close to them.

But is there something more to being an empath? How can we clearly separate an empath from a person that's just slightly more sensitive than the ordinary?

According to Dr. Elaine Aron, highly sensitive people (or HSPs, as she calls them) share a lot of traits with the empath from being easily excitable to needing time alone to unwind or responding differently to normal stimuli such as noise, smells, and light. Empaths also tend to be rather introverted, like HSPs, even if that's not a ground rule. Nevertheless, the difference between the two types of personalities is clear, and that is the spiritual side of being an empath. They are like modern "sensing machines," able to detect the unseen energies of their environments and to manipulate them to some extent. They can fill themselves up with feelings and emotions to a point that they can't even tell for sure where their own emotions end and where the absorbed energy begins. HSPs might have the empathy and the sensitivities that empaths do, but their spiritual potential is nowhere near them.

If you still have doubts regarding your inclusion in the empath category, then don't fret, because Dr. Judith Orloff created the perfect way to know for sure: a quiz. Eight simple questions to mull over in your free time:

- Have people tagged you as being too sensible or overly emotional?

- Do you tend to unknowingly "borrow" the negative feelings of your friends?

- Is it easy for you to get emotionally hurt?

- Do crowds cause your energy levels to drop drastically? And if yes, do you feel "refreshed" after spending some time alone?

- Are you sensitive to noises, lights, or smells? Does excessive talking make you feel uneasy?

- Do you prefer to be in control of when and where you go by using your own vehicle as a transportation method?

- Is emotional stress a problem that you face quite often and that you find hard to cope with?

- Do being in an intimate relationship frightens you because of the emotional implications of it? Or rather, do you have a fear of being "swallowed up" in someone else's emotions and losing your identity?

If you have a positive answer for more than three of these questions, then you are indeed an empath. If you found yourself in only three of the questions, then you are at least part empath. It is very important for you to know exactly what "terminology" applies to you because it leads to a better understanding of yourself. And knowing yourself opens up the path for self-improvements and getting the most out of your life.

Besides giving people an easy way of finding out

whether they truly are empaths or just partially included in the farther side of the empathy spectrum, Dr. Orloff also managed to pinpoint some definite traits.

1. Empaths are emotional sponges—they are so in sync with the people around them that they become directly dependent on their moods and feelings. Emotions like sadness and anger will be maximized by the empath and will affect his mental and emotional state in a negative way. On the other hand, positive emotions will ensure the happiness and well-being of the empath.

2. Empaths have an intuition like no other— thanks to their high spirituality, empaths are born with a highly honed gut feeling. The way they live their life and asses different situations is always through their intuition, which needs to be developed from an early age.

3. Empaths are overly sensitive—being open comes with the disadvantage that anything can touch them, and subsequently hurt them.

People are often annoyed by their inability to handle their own emotions.

4. Empaths have a tendency to be introverted—they internalize everything and being out too much drains their energy. They prefer to stay away from crowds and be in control of who they interact with and for how long.

5. Empaths need space—without some alone time, they find it hard to survive, and they are prone to emotional burnouts.

6. Nature is a refuge for empaths—they often need to escape the stress and fast pace of our society, and nature does a great job at replenishing their dusty batteries.

7. Improved senses—because they experience excitable elements in different ways that the usual people, they are easily affected by stimuli such as smells, noises, and lights.

8. Empath fear intimate relationships—it is not that they can't commit to someone else, but they find it harder to keep their individuality in a couple since they can be easily "drowned"

by someone else's feelings.

9. Empaths don't know when to stop giving—they are born with the feeling that they have to "save the world" so they end up going more than an extra mile to reach out to someone in need. So much that they compromise their own well-being by absorbing the negative feelings of others.

10. Empaths are easy targets for energy drainers—people that feed on the energies of others will find the best victim potential in the empath. That includes, but is not limited to: people that make a drama out of everything, the forever victim, the talker that never stops talking and the narcissist that thrives by diminishing others worth.

Now that we have a better understanding of what being an empath means, we can also come to the conclusion that an empath is vulnerable. Not only can they be easily influenced by the misfortunes of others, but they adapt harder to the stress-ridden, fast pace of today's society, and they can be preyed upon by selfish opportunists. It's fair to say that empaths have it harder than they should, and they are in a desperate need of finding ways to protect themselves and cope with the world. Dr. Orloff that identifies herself as being an empath shared that her methods include *"setting fierce time management, setting limits and boundaries with draining people, meditation to calm and center myself and going out into nature."* That's a lot of work to simply survive on a daily basis, but a certain amount of effort is required for any empath that wishes to have a happy and healthy life.

Empaths may have a lot of setbacks, but their qualities can't be easily ignored either. They are excellent friends, dedicated listeners and overall big-hearted persons with a kindness that's off the charts. All they need is good solutions to keep themselves afloat—finding that miracle formula to improve their lives, just like Dr. Orloff did. We will explore together different problems and situations that empaths have a hard time dealing with, in order to find some effective solutions.

Keep in mind that any issue can be overcome, with the right approach and mindset.

Chapter 2. Being a Highly Sensitive Person in Today's Society

Our society is at its peak if we are talking about scientific breakthroughs, opportunities, and comfort. We don't have nearly as many worries as our ancestors had, regarding our health and safety, and we sure do have a sense of freedom like never before. However, it would be a stretch to say that our generation is happier than generations past.

Why is that?

It's because of expectations. We have so many possibilities and opportunities that it's expected of us to live the ultimate dream: a perfect job, the perfect life partner, the perfect house and so on. The pressure of society is so high that all this need to have it all "the right way" turn into pure stress. And we know by now that stress and highly sensitive people don't really get along like old pals.

It's not like people from the past were not emotional. We have plenty of extraordinary pieces of art that perfectly show just how expressive and sensible they were. The only reason why it was not a recognized issue back then it's that, there were other pressing matters to focus on. Famine, illness, wars—those were their worries and the highlights of our history.

But now, we have the time to asses our mental health. We have the opportunity to center our attention on getting to know ourselves, in order for us to reach a real state of happiness. That's why it seems that people now are more sensible and fragile than they ever were before. Here we are in the era ruled by anxiety, depression, emotional drain, and burnout.

Let's focus on the more general challenges that highly sensitive people face in today's society. One of the biggest issue they have to take on is the possibility of being rejected by society. Why? Because they are in all aspects different. And those that stick out from the crowd are often frowned upon and judged. Sensitive people are not simply driven by a desire to survive and gain some fancy status to hide their insecurities behind. They use their finely tuned empathy to see far beyond social norms, and their eagerness to help, or be helpful, may simply become sources of annoyance for type A personalities. In this competition for greatness, they are seen as gullible sheep—people that don't have the guts necessary to pull the bull by its horns to achieve success.

Another issue that may turn into a cause for praying eyes rolling is the empaths fear of intimate relationships. Let's face it—society will always judge people that are alone. People have a very clear idea of how life is supposed to be and work out, and they consider anyone that does not follow that narrative to be a "failure." If you're in your late twenties and you're not at least preparing to get married, then there must be something wrong with you. You, in a way or another, have proven to be undesirable as a life partner. You lack something; therefore, you must be a miserable person. That's kind of how people think it, whether they say it aloud or not. It's funny that we've come so far as a society just to remain stuck in some "social beliefs" that don't apply anymore. Not being in a relationship does not diminish your value as a person, in any way shape or form. If only society agreed to that, the world would be a better place.

The list of challenges doesn't end here. Unfortunately, things can go sour from early childhood. Because a highly sensitive child is different, it requires a different parental approach for healthy development. They are able to understand the fact that they are not like their peers, but they don't have a clear concept of their self. Likewise, the other children are able to tell apart those unique, sensitive little ones, and they tend to avoid them, again from lack of understanding how to socialize with them. Also, parents can misunderstand their child and often try to "put a label" on their weird comportment. From ADHD to narcissistic or borderline personality, all those can be "tags" for a parent that doesn't grasp the real identity of his child. Such approaches only lead to the child shutting in his feeling and completely internalizing them, which is obviously unhealthy for a fragile little emotional firecracker.

Even the simple things are rough on the empath. Socializing needs to be limited and somewhat controlled because highly sensitive people can't survive in crowded noise environments too long and they also have a tendency to overthink anything. Hand gestures, body language, tones, they pay attention to everything and they easily transform a normal interaction into a chess game of trying to get into the other person's mind and read his moves. But there are even more things that make socializing sound like a torturous feat. Empaths are sensitive to noises, and the concept of someone yelling at them is almost nauseating. It can feel like being physically admonished, even if the tone is just slightly raised than on a regular basis. Also, highly sensitive people hate to disappoint others so many time they end up agreeing to do things even if, deep down they would rather not.

Empaths are naturally emotional, so the way they respond to things is rather different from regular people. They have a strong reaction to both positive and negative things, this emotional outburst only deepening the concept of being somewhat isolated or ostracized from other people. Jokes can strike deep chords even if they were meant in good fun. Empaths often feel exhausted, on an emotional level, because they do like to take in the feelings of other people. As a consequence of that, having a hectic sleeping program can easily tip over a sensitive person's life. Sleep is an ultimate necessity for any human being, but empaths might require some extra doses as they battle both mental and emotional fatigue on a daily basis. Since they experience the whole world differently, sensitive people can't even fully enjoy a vacation because of little aspects like crowds, the novelty of the environment or even the requirement of sleeping in a new bed.

All those aside, we can't ignore the value of highly sensitive people in our society. We are in desperate need of kindhearted people, now more than ever. They have the power to shift our minds away from our everyday problems and fill us up with motivation and newfound energy. Their creativeness brings beauty to the world. Their innovative ideas make unsolvable issues seem like trivialities. Being a highly sensitive person is not some crippling disease, only a twist on how the brain works, even if some people mistakenly believe that a high sensitivity automatically puts you on the autism spectrum. According to Dr. Elaine Aron, there is no real correlation between autism and being an empath. Twenty percent of the population falls in the category of "highly sensitive," and none of those individuals experience Asperger's syndrome. The distress that autistic people feel when faced with stimuli is because of improper use of sensory information, while highly sensitive people's emotional response comes from a deep mental process.

Although, some mental health issues were indeed linked with being overly sensitive, such as depression and anxiety, but there's no rule to it. It's more of a higher risk case rather than a fixed scenario.

A highly sensitive person is prone to be stigmatized, ostracized, and judged by society, just for the fact that they don't fit in their ideals. It's a sad reality that will take decades or eras to change if it ever will. Still, it's important for any highly sensitive person to know exactly what they are up against for them to find out the best way of dealing with it. Any empath can become an active, high functional part of their community if they are willing to work on their flaws and hone their qualities.

To survive in a society so eager to label and judge you, it takes a little bit of guidance and some effort. At the end of the day, the whole world can benefit from the gifts of a highly sensitive person, as long as they know how to accept them and value them as they are.

Chapter 3. How to Stop Emotional Overload

The feeling of being overwhelmed is unfortunately very common nowadays because we have all the favoring factors simply laying around. There's plenty of stress to go round for everybody and if we mix that with some personal issues any person in their right mind would feel the need to let out some emotional steam. That's where a highly sensitive person can come in and save the day for someone.

But what happens when the good empath has had his share of the world's negative emotions? How can he avoid the trap of drowning in unresolved and unexpressed emotions and why are highly sensitive people more prone to this emotional burnout?

The why is simple enough. It's in an empath's nature to absorb the feelings of others, as "bad" as they can be, a situation that usually ends up with the healer itself needing some "emotional treatment." Deborah Ward, a journalist, and an HSP describes her experience after taking in the negative emotions of one of her coworkers: "I was so full of emotion I was shaking. My hands were sweating. My heart was pounding. I was on the verge of tears. For the rest of the day, I felt exhausted and needed to be alone." This is a very good example of how easy it is for empaths to be deeply affected by the emotions of others, and to slip into an emotional overload scenario.

A good strategy that many empaths go for is trying to prevent the "emotional bomb" from forming rather than fighting it off when it happens. This method allows for having more control over one's life and choosing a proactive solution instead of going with the current of life. Prevention comes in many shapes and forms and varies from life choices to effective little "tricks."

A practice that helped many empaths is awareness. That itself is a relative concept which either focuses on the sensorial perception of our environments or to the internal state. Both types come in handy for the empath. To be aware of your own thoughts and feeling helps highly sensitive people separate their own emotions from the energies and feelings that they "pick up on the road." Also, if a person is grounded in his surroundings and is therefore aware of the existent stimuli, he can come up with a better way of assimilating them, without feeling overwhelmed.

Another concept that helps with prevention is energy. Empaths have great spiritual potential, and they are able to read and feel energies. Even more than reading, they can also unconsciously feed on the energies that surround them. Energy comes in both positive and negative forms. Positive energies are generated by feelings such as love, forgiveness, and kindness while negative ones come from sadness, anger, and so on. Those energies can come from people or can reside in different places and areas. Think of energy like some sort of baggage that you can carry around or leave somewhere. Empaths have the ability to pick up this baggage and make it their own, even if that might not be in their best interest. Being aware of those energies can help a highly sensitive person choose which baggage to pick up and which to let go, avoiding an overload situation.

Sometimes other people's problems can't be solved by an outside person no matter how well he or she might understand the said problem. Empaths tend to take the world's problems into their own hands, and not being able to find a solution can drive them to experience an emotional burnout. As hard as it is for an empath to accept, you can't save everybody. People need to learn from their personal mistakes and grow out of them. No amount of advice can compare to banging your own head against the wall and having to deal with the situation that ensues. So empaths need to learn to let people have their own experiences and stop taking their failures as a personal mishap. Do your part by adding positive feeling and energies into the mixt then detach yourself emotionally from the situation.

Finding a balance can also be the key to an easier life. Every person in a way or another is looking for a form of balance: personal life versus work, a healthy diet going against sweet treats, and so on. Empaths, on the other hand, need to find the equilibrium between their inner and outer life. There's so much going on in a sensitive's person mind that it can be easy at times to fall into the abyss of thoughts and expressed feelings. Awareness can be a strong tool to keep this balance from crashing down. That being said, every person has its own definition of a healthy balance. It comes back to you the responsibility to find the thing that helps you unwind and to tell the good energies from the bad ones in order to minimize the unhealthy "absorptions."

As I mentioned before, there are also clever tricks that can keep you on the safe side of things, with a little bit of practice. Pay close attention to your emotional responses to different situations and pinpoint what the exact trigger of it was. Julie Bjelland, a self-development expert, believes that by being able to take note of the things which produce an unhealthy emotional response you can create a "pause and reflect ability." This is a step by step technique that unfolds as follows:

1. You start noticing some things that could be your triggers, but nothing is sure yet.

2. You become aware of your triggers and start understanding that you can control the response you give. At first, this will end up in the same way you are already used to it going—with an emotional overload ready to burst, but you will slowly start realizing that you have a choice. You can create a completely new response that won't compromise your emotional stability.

3. At last, you manage to achieve the "pause and

reflect" skill. You know your triggers, and you can get yourself out of the mess, relatively unharmed, by being able to assess your situation and choosing a course of action voluntarily.

Julie Bjelland doesn't stop there with her witty ideas. Adding to the control over your emotional response, another great help for the empath is the ability to switch on your cognitive brain, which basically means focusing on hard facts instead of personal emotions. Going down the emotional rabbit hole will most likely result in getting to Emotional Overload Land. The trick is to understand the emotion you are feeling and slowly but surely taking it apart piece by piece. Let's say you are feeling insecure. The best thing to do is pump up your cognitive side by finding facts to contra attack the emotion. Remember the times when you succeeded to do something that you did not believe you could. Bring back from memory lane all the praises that you got, all the times when others appreciated you for both your accomplishments and simple presence. There's hardly any place for insecurities when you have all this bucket-load of arguments that prove your worth.

So prevention is a blessing in disguise. But what do you do when you are caught right in the middle of an overwhelming emotional episode? Andrea Brandt, a family therapist, offers up some familiar solutions. Awareness comes back to the plate, but in another form known as "mindfulness." The term refers to living actively in the moment and being conscious of your every experience. In that way, you can fight off emotions, right as they come at you. Deep breaths help you stay focused without retreating into your mind trap while some motivational quotes can help you realize the temporary nature of emotions and the power you have over them. There's plenty of quotes to choose from, and it's highly indicated to go and pick out those that really speak to you on an emotional level, be it from specialty books or simply from the web. Aside "mindfulness" Andrea Brandt places emotional control. "Feeling the emotion isn't the same thing as reacting to it," she presses. What matters is the response you choose to give. Flashback to Julie Bjelland's "pause and reflect" technique, right?

As a conclusion, different methods can both stop or outright prevent emotional overload. Or to be more specific about it, any method on its own can get you out of that bad mental state, but by practicing it, again and again, it can also become a strong means of prevention. Knowing to work your energies, being aware, willingly choosing a response to an emotional message, maintaining a balance, all those will change your life for the better and offer you ways to protect yourself in your quest of saving others.

Chapter 4. How to Cope with Anxiety in Big Crowds

Anxiety is no stranger to highly sensitive people. It's a natural mental response to the overwhelming amount of stimulation that empaths get from their environments. That mixed in with all the emotional baggage that they end up picking up from other people, and the formula is done. Purely concentrated anxiety, ready to shake your mind and soul and leave you wondering if you are good enough for this world.

So What's Anxiety and How Does That Manifest for Highly Sensitive People?

There are many ways to define anxiety, from a state of mind to an accumulation of feelings such as fear, irritation, the inability to focus on something, or more easily "being on edge." It's a disastrous cocktail for a person that already experiences deep emotional responses to even the smallest things. However, we must not overlook the fact that a lot of people deal with anxiety on a daily basis, even if they don't have strong empathy. It's something that can affect anyone, regardless of age, sex, or mental strength. The point is finding ways to cope with anxiety or, as some say, ways to make it your own.

When regarding the anxious feelings of her highly sensitive son, Sheryl Paul, an accomplished author talks about the importance of going with the flow of feelings. She believes that the only way to break free from your fears is by having the courage to "feel them" and accept them as they are—a part of yourself. Her point is that the emotional response that you are caught in is not shameful or an example of weakness, but a normal way of reacting to something in your life. So instead of denying them, it's best to go through them and let them pass, this process turning you into a better, stronger person.

Barbara Markway, an experienced psychologist, also shares some of those ideas like accepting anxiety as something that comes naturally and how those feelings must be experienced in order to break free from the "emotional hurricane." More than that, in her opinion we must be aware of the fact that our anxious thoughts and feelings do not defy the state of reality. Anxiety works with your insecurities, fears, and weaknesses, which is why it's so easy to get manipulated into believing the worst about your situation. But following a negative train of thought is a habit, and, like all habits, it can be changed. And the only way to break this chain of negativity is by focusing on realistic thinking—based on fact, not suppositions. Breathing deeply can likewise help you ease out of the anxious episode. Mrs. Markway proposes the following exercise: "While lying in bed, rest your hands on your abdomen. Breathing deeply through your nose to a count of four, let your abdomen rise as you inhale. Your chest should remain still. As you breathe out—two a count of four—your abdomen should flatten. Slow your breathing to eight breaths per minute." There's no harm in giving breathing a chance.

Deborah Ward, a journalist, and an empath we have already talked about before brings in her own ideas about coping with anxiety. For her, recognizing the sign of anxiety come with the package of being able to handle them in a proper way. She too warns about the danger of falling in the trap of your own overflowingly negative imagination and recommends trying relaxation techniques. The obvious examples would be meditation or yoga as anyone instantly pairs them up with "relaxation," but it's more about doing something that helps you unwind. Reading, listening to music, going for a walk in the park, they all count, so don't be afraid to explore until you finally set your eyes on the ultimate technique.

Leaving generalities aside, one of the biggest challenges any empath faces is crowds. The cacophony of noises, emotions, smells, can really tickle all the anxious bones in a highly sensitive person, leaving them unable to deal with the abundance of jittery thoughts.

Going for a roundabout way of minimalizing "crowd suffocation" Dr. Orloff, another familiar figure, made up a short list with some pieces of advice:

- Manage your activities and plans in order to avoid an overload of stressing scenarios.

- Hone both your native intuition and your spiritual awareness to protect yourself from sensorial triggers.

- Maintain a balance in your life and focus on being both mentally and physically healthy.

- Be aware of the sensorial inputs that could lead to emotional overload.

- Create long-term strategies to cope with anxious situations like protecting yourself from harmful energies and not being afraid to step away from tumultuous situations.

For those that are looking for an easier way of easing their discomfort caused by crowds, there are plenty of tactics that can be implemented. A very effective one is making sure that you have someone with you when you are confronting with a social situation such as conglomerations of people. It could be a friend, a family member or your significant other, that does not really matter. What does matter though is, letting that person know your fears and issues, and teaching them how to react in an emergency situation—like a panic attack or the impending need of getting away from it all.

Additionally, setting everyday goals for yourself can also improve your situation. The goals need to be as achievable as possible since the purpose is slowly getting used to a social situation rather than power forcing through it. By getting exposed to crowds, for shorts periods of time, as often as you are able to, you end up gradually getting over your initial anxiety. The practice is called desensitization, and it is commonly used to treat all sorts of fears. The results are overwhelmingly positive.

Here's something that we need to take into consideration: we all have limits. There are things that we can and can't do. Knowing our boundaries is an important part of better understanding ourselves and coming up with the best solution to our problems. Boundaries are understandable, but using the kind of techniques that were mentioned above, your comfort area will give way and expand. Your limits will change and reach new, more agreeable levels. But that must come in time, with a lot of practice and effort. Don't try to force your limits. It does not work that way, and you will only end up doing more damage than good. Be aware of your limits and be patient with them. It will get better.

A usual reason why highly sensitive people tend to get anxious in crowds is that they find that situation as risky. After all, there are so many things that could go wrong for them, so their feelings are completely justified. However, as Chloe Carmichael, a renowned psychologist, advises: "You might tell yourself, *you already thought this through and made the choice to be here, and the best thing you can do right now is to focus on having fun or doing what you came here to do.*" Rather than focusing on all that can go sour, it would be a nice change to simply go through the experience and see what you get out of it.

We are the creators of our own anxieties, and we do have the ability to overcome them. We all have the potential to surpass our fears, all we need is some guidance and a whole bunch of dedication.

Chapter 5. How to Cope with Hypersensitivity on a Spiritual Level

Empaths are spiritual beings, whether they like it or not. It's simply in their nature to be in tune with everything and feel other's experiences as their own. Many even believe that hypersensitivity is a tell-tale sign of a soul that's ready to evolve beyond the realm of ordinary life. If an empath develops his spirituality accordingly, he will start perceiving life in a whole different way while also discovering hidden creativity. This "tuning in with their soul" allows highly sensitive people to stop getting stuck in the problems and issues of humanity but instead find ways to change for the better both their lives and the lives of those around them.

One would say that there are only benefits in further exploring the dormant potential of your soul, but, as it usually goes with life, that's easier said than done. Hypersensitivity is hard to deal with for an untrained spirit. So one must find ways to see beyond the trees and discover the forest.

Starting from the bottom, let's see what are some factors that may block you from further investigating your spiritual side, in order to get a firm grasp on your senses and how they affect you.

Initial Disappointment

A lot of people start this journey of self-discovery by having a lot of expectations. You wish that it would all be easy as a pickle and that in no time you'd be on your way to resolving all the problems of our century. But starting on something new with having little to no idea of what you are supposed to do, never works like that. You have the tool that you need, your native ability to sense the world and absorb its energies, but you don't know yet how to differentiate those fields of concentrated emotions. It's better to start off with no expectations, just a blank page that's ready to accept any picture that your soul will paint on it.

A Lack of Patience

Always being on the lookout for something great and bigger than yourself will get you nowhere. You end up second-guessing yourself and your potential, which lead to anxiety and an overall sense of restlessness. It's not easy to understand such a wide concept like spirituality and how you can use it to your benefit, but you will get there. Patience is one of your biggest allies in the trial of evolving as a person and a member of a community.

A Messy Environment

Feng shui, a well-known Chinese pseudoscience, puts a lot of weight on the state of cleanness of the space you reside in. It is said that the soul needs to be in harmony with its surroundings, so, in other words, a messy space creates a messy spirit. People thrive in clean, organized environments, there is no denying that, and a good idea is to apply that to all the spaces you can, such as your office.

Unhealthy Diet

Anthelme Brillat-savarin once wrote, "Tell me what you eat, and I will tell you what you are," widely known as the most simplistic, "You are what you eat." Not to be taken literally, the phrase refers to how our diet influence both our physical and mental health. In spiritual terms, everything that you put in your body as a means of fueling it will affect your "vibrations." Each food item comes with its own vibration that could either lift your energy or sink it low to the ground. Some clear examples of "bad foods" include processed food (such as fast food and canned goods), unhealthy oils (like margarine), frozen foods, and sugary foods (especially those that have artificial sweeteners). Also up on the bad category, we have coffee and alcohol, substances which deeply affect the state of the mind in both good and bad ways.

Overthinking

That's one of the biggest hurdles since all empaths tend to mull over every single detail, even when there is no need to do so. You can't really benefit from all the positive energy lying around when you're busy stressing over some minuscule mistake you've done or whatever thought you choose to obsess about. Live in the moment and be aware of yourself and your surroundings.

Now we've seen what may keep us from strengthening our spiritual powers, and that surely helps a lot with a better apprehension of the overwhelming output that empaths get from the world. There are also ways to protect your spirit from getting emotionally overloaded (for example, moving physically away from a source of negative energy, even if you are in fear of offending someone). It's wonderful to consider someone else's feelings, but that does not make them more important than your well-being. Having some distance will ease up the empathy levels and give you a well-deserved break.

Don't be afraid to set

some ground rules and limits regarding your interactions. Saying "no" is a completely valid option and you should not feel bad for interrupting a conversation that emotionally drains you. All socializing should be done in healthy measures that you are comfortable with. If you do end up stuck in someone else's "energy field" try shifting the focus back to your own person. Slowly breathing usually does the trick, but sometimes it's also handy to mentally visualize yourself getting disconnected from the negative energies.

Furthermore, try some quick meditation sessions if you start feeling overwhelmed by a social situation such as a party or gathering. A few minutes is all you need to get yourself centered back on your own heart and sorting out any unwanted energies that might have slipped your barriers. An opportunistically empty room—a bathroom or a garden, depending on what's available to you—can become effective meditation centers. You don't need anything fancy, just a quiet place that allows for a handful of relaxing minutes.

And the cherry to top it all is, planning ahead. Dr. Judith Orloff recommends any empath to settle for five of their most emotionally stressful situations and come up with a "scheme" to make them easy to handle. Her examples include sticking to your maximum hours of socializing that you're comfortable with, not being afraid to say no, finding the quietest place to occupy in a crowded area (and also eating a hearty meal beforehand, as that helps physically "ground" you) and actively dealing with the scents that upset you (by staying near ventilation sources or taking plenty of fresh air breaks). Having a plan will save you a lot of trouble and will surely make your spirit more susceptible to successfully dealing with your hyper-load of senses.

Being a highly sensitive person automatically means that you are more gifted spiritually than others. That being said, it also warns you that you have to put on some extra effort if you want your spirit to cope with your ever-changing emotional levels. Hone your native abilities and cut out the things that affect you in a negative way. The three Ps—practice, patience, and planning—will get you on the right track.

Chapter 6. How to Channel Your Emotions and Hypersensitivity into Healing Yourself

Throughout our lives, we face many situations that leave us with long-lasting negative effects. Call them traumas or just bad episodes from our past—those change us in ways we are not even aware of, crippling our ability to connect with the world that surrounds us. However, any shattered thing can be put back together or turned into something new, a fresh concept that fits in the place of what we lost. Anyone has the ability to heal themselves, and empath may even have a bonus advantage with their strong spiritual and emotional nature. There are plenty of ways in which highly sensitive people can use their concentrated emotional side to heal the pains of the past.

From here on let's explore a few ideas: how can you heal yourself by channeling your emotions, what's the link between the biochemistry happening in our organism and emotional healing, how can we get rid of unwanted emotional baggage and what hidden benefit lies behind emotional wounds. Each brings a new dimension to the issue at hand and helps us understand the ins and outs of self-healing and acceptance.

How to Emotionally Heal Yourself

Many times when we picture "healing" our mind immediately goes to therapy and medication. Sure, they do have their benefits, and many people desperately need them. But Eric R. Meisel, a psychotherapist and writer, thinks there might be other things out there that can tip the balance in our favor.

- Deciding who you want to be—our environments changes our initial personality and behavior. This is a normal thing that happens on a subconscious level. However, there comes a point in our lives when we must take the saddles and make an actual choice regarding what we want to become. Work toward being less prone to emotional distress by taking a step back to assess your situation, becoming less self-critical, focusing on positive feelings, and so on.

- Don't lose your identity—it's easy for sensitive people to go overboard in the quest of pleasing the people in their lives. Still, you are your own person. You have things that you like and things that you don't. You have limits and boundaries. That is completely fine. Don't let others dictate how or who you should be, based on their wishes.

- Find meaning in your life, or create one for yourself—a meaning is something that's different for every person, based on their beliefs and life perceptions. Everybody has their own definition of what and how a meaningful life should be. What matters most is making sure that you do see a purpose for everything that you do. You have the ability to make even a small little thing seem meaningful. Having a purpose and living a meaningful life reduces a lot of the existential anxiety factor, leaving more space for happiness and calmness.

- A culture of love—empaths need alone time in order to survive, but there's no question that they are the happiest when they can go out and share the love they feel toward the world. Just as you show kindness to others, you must let them love you back and take care of you from time to time. Even a dedicated healer might be in need of saving now and then.

- Control your thoughts—they are the blade that cut the deepest in our souls, and they are purely fabricated by us, almost never showcasing reality. Emotional burdens get far easier when you don't go picking at them with your negative chains of thinking.

- Create favorable circumstances for yourself— environments matter. As mentioned before, what surrounds us ends up shaping us as persons. If you go out and willingly put yourself in situations that are harming for you or you let the wrong kind of people in your life, how are you supposed to grow as a person and heal? Improving your circumstances will greatly affect your emotions for the better. No healing is going to happen in a dark, moldy, decrepit environment. You control what type of energies surround you.

- Don't get latched on the past—you've been there, you've done that, now it's over. It's been over for quite some time now, so why not let it go? We as people have the bad habit of attaching ourselves to bad experiences, unconsciously relieving them again and again, not giving them enough time to heal. Feeling an emotion is important, but more so is letting it go when it has no more meaning in your life.

Biochemistry and Emotional Healing

What's the link between molecules and emotions? Believe it or not, we have special types of molecules in our body that are directly responsible for making the body react to feelings such as fear or happiness. If we can understand the relationship between our emotions and the way our body responds to them, we are left with the wonderful possibility of healing ourselves by holding on to the healthy emotional signals. Meaning that by channeling a specific type of emotional content you can influence your body's chemistry toward "healing."

This whole talk of molecules is not the easiest thing, and I'm not here trying to prepare the reader for a biochemistry doctorate. I will just present a few examples of this link between emotion and science, in order to help you see the possible benefits that this knowledge could bring you.

Acetylcholine is a neurotransmitter is a wide variety of effects. It helps you sleep, it enhances your ability to learn, and it is known to increase emotional health by allowing you to enjoy life. A reduced level of this molecule is associated with a lack of creativity and insomnia, while an excessive level contributes to feeling anxious and restless. You can balance out your body's acetylcholine by meditating, recalling an emotion you rarely encounter in your life until you feel it or by picturing a feeling you never experienced.

Serotonin is another neurotransmitter that might sound familiar since it is known to have a direct correlation with mood. Low serotonin might cause negative feelings while a high level of it leads to feeling happy and overall content. It is widely believed that an imbalance in serotonin's levels are one of the factors that lead to depression and anxiety, although that is not set in stone. To balance it, try things like reducing the stress you are subjected to, meeting your natural body needs, getting massages or other relaxation techniques and exposing yourself to natural light, in healthy doses (vitamin D helps with the production of serotonin).

So before focusing on self-healing maybe consider what your body needs and what's your body's state? Is your emotional input helping your organism heal? Are you indulging in a healthy lifestyle that keeps your hormonal level on the floating line, ready to help you? Remember, positive feelings create positive responses, and both science and spirituality can live in peace together as powerful allies.

Emotional Release

Sometimes, the best way to heal yourself is by letting go. Emotions that are kept inside for too long have the tendency of going "stale." In those situations, it's better to channel them on the outside of your body, so the void left can be filled with fresher, more positive energies.

Deepak Chopra, MD, identifies seven simple steps in which you can release the emotional load. Those are meant to be part of a meditation process in which you visualize your emotions and tune your spirit to them.

1. Identify the emotion you are feeling by understanding its nature and what has created it.

2. Observe how it has affected you both mentally and physically.

3. Live the respective emotion and express it, let yourself experience it thoroughly, even write it down on paper if that helps you.

4. Accept the consequences that the emotion has

on your mind and body, and take responsibility for feeling that way. You brought that emotion onto yourself, and you are the only one who can take it away.

5. Allow the emotion to leave your body, in your own unique way like dancing it out, singing it away or burning the paper in which you've written it.

6. Visualize yourself talking with the cause of your emotional distress (a projection of a person involved) and sharing your healing process with it. It's a way of assuring yourself that you are over it and you will not fall into the same negative patterns again.

7. Celebrate your accomplishments as you like. Treating yourself to some of your favorite foods, going out with friends, whatever makes you feel relaxed and happy. By this point, you've managed to turn a bad experience into a spiritual opportunity, you've earned it.

Mary Jo Rapini, a counselor, believes that voicing your feelings also works out. It's a method of putting it out there instead of internalizing it. Likewise, she recommends acting on your emotions. If you feel like crying then do so. Feel like screaming in frustration or letting out a monumental *sigh*? Go ahead! Don't hold anything that itches to burst out of your soul.

When you're unconsciously holding on to some emotional baggage, your body will be quick to bring out the red flags. Body functions are affected, and pains start to magically appear, without no apparent cause whatsoever. The most common signs of internalized emotional problems are insomnia, anxiety, depression, stomach, neck or back pain, sudden weight loss or gain, and rheumatoid arthritis. Even if you can treat the physical problem, you will not necessarily feel better until the real emotional issue is sorted out.

The Bright Side of Emotional Wounds

As painful as it is to sort out your feeling and heal the damage left behind, it's not all bad. With every experience, you become stronger and wiser. The pain goes away, but your scars are there to remind you of the challenges you faced and conquered. You paved the way toward avoiding further emotional problems and, thanks to your experience you can now help others that are on the same healing path as you once were.

You know that you can handle anything, and you become more open to accepting the feelings and living them as they are. They trigger a complex transformation in yourself which furthermore cultivates a movement of love both related to your own person and to others.

Bad experiences aren't here to stop us or make our lives miserable. They just give us the chance to grow as people and as kind, compassionate beings, focused on forgiveness and acceptance, shifting the balance of the world from negative to positive.

Chapter 7. Healing Others While Protecting Your Energy

For empaths, helping others is not always a matter of conscious choice. It's a calling—a soul calling. It is not just a chance to lend someone a helping hand, but a unique opportunity to grow as a person and better understand who you are. It can help you find your way in life and a purpose bigger than yourself.

When you answer to a soul call you don't know what you'll get. You might come out of the experience stronger and more confident in your spiritual powers. But you could also feel emotionally overloaded or drained of all your positive energies. Because let's face it, empaths are easily taken advantage of and if you don't know how to protect yourself successfully while trying to lift someone up, you might end up sinking with them into the sea of sorrow. It's all about finding a good balance, which will allow you to invest your energies into the things that actually matter.

So how can you protect yourself while also using your gift for the greater good of humanity? Sylvia Salow, a well-known life coach, thinks she found the formula to this complicated equation.

Write Down Your Emotions

Journaling suits empaths like a glove. Energies tend to transform when they are put on paper, shifting into something that you can benefit from. It's a great way to release negative energies and to maintain some sort of stability in your life.

Meditate

There's no surprise with this one. I've mentioned meditation times and times again in this book because it's such a vital habit to pick up for any person that wishes to reach a state of calmness like no other. For highly sensitive people meditation, it's a means of not losing connection with their own feeling and emotions. It's easier not to get lost in someone else's drama when you are close to your heart and you are aware of your own experiences.

Kundalini Yoga

Kundalini is a form of energy that Hindus people believe to be located at the base of the spine. The purpose of this type of yoga is to awaken this energy through meditation, special breathing techniques along with chanting mantras. It's a great method of protecting your energies, and practitioners described the experience as feeling like "an electric current running along their spines."

Don't Collect Foreign Energies

It's nearly impossible for an empath to not stumble upon a whole bunch of energies, and unconsciously pick them up. The tricky part is to be aware of when you are doing that and release those energies that don't belong to you back into nature. The last thing you want to do is put them on a shelf and start collecting them. You'll run out of space very fast, and you'll end up suddenly overwhelmed by a piece of emotional baggage that's not even your own.

Unplug from the Emotional Fountain

Most of the time if not always, prevention is preferred in the place of dealing with something. And sometimes that means you have to detach from some people's emotions because they are not ready to be helped. When you feel the need to solve someone else's issues or to heal them, you create that line of communication between you two—a line that goes both ways and might get you a big dose of the person's negative energy. Keep in mind that we all have problems that we need to learn how to cope with on our own. It's a step-by-step program that takes time. When they are ready to be helped, you will know.

Avoiding Malevolent Energies

I've mentioned before that empaths are magnets for some questionable types of people. Those are called "energetic vampires," and they are selfish, incredibly self-centered people that just want to "feed" on your emotions. There are also people who harbor such strong negative feelings regarding yourself that they unwillingly fill you up with "bad" energies. In those situations, it's better to just cut them out of your life if possible. If not, limit your interactions with them. Keep it short and brief, and no one will suffer. Your well-being matters!

Have Time for Yourself

Empaths require frequent breaks from the world in order to keep their sanity and emotional stability. But even when away, a highly sensitive person will still think about all the people that require their presence and as a result of that might feel guilty or selfish. That's an unhealthy way of thinking! Empaths are emotional sponges that need time to "shake it all off." There's no way you'll be of any help to people until you are successfully detached of your "old" emotional load. So leave the guilt at the door and just relax. Allow yourself that.

An Emotional Vacuum Cleaner

It's a quirky method that Sylvia Salow practices frequently and, for her, it is very effective. The idea is to visualize in your mind a vacuum cleaner (or any absorbent item like a sponge, it's your mind your rules) that takes away all your negative energies or overflowing feelings. With some practice, you can learn to use this any time you please, even if you're right in the middle of a conversation. It could work out as a great trick not only for protecting your energies but also for avoiding an emotional overload.

Keeping Your Shield Up

Similar to the vacuum, this technique also requires some visualizing. Many believe that by creating a protective shape around you, the negative energies can't reach you and therefore you are safe. However, Sylvia warns about a general misconception. This "shield" should not be fully closed, completely encapsulating you inside. Energies are ever flowing. They need to move in and out of your body in a constant empirical waltz. So leave a way out for them when imagining your protection layer, either at the top or bottom, so your body is covered. Like so, you are safe but also able to move your own energies around in order to keep a healthy balance.

Crystals

A tale as old as time is the potent healing power of gemstones. There's a wide array of colorful items to choose from. Let's quickly go through a top of protective gemstones by Krista Mitchell, a crystal healing expert.

1. Black tourmaline—it is good for general protection against harmful energies.

2. Jet—it absorbs some of the energies thrown your way, a great survival tool for any empath.

3. Labradorite—it protects you against malevolent intents and psychic attacks.

4. Fluorite—it hides and protects your energetic aura against more serious threats.

5. Blue kyanite—it helps you keep your head clear of anxieties, confusions, and insecurities.

6. Black obsidian—it's a powerful healer that gets rid of dark energies that might pester you.

7. Apache tear—it's another healer stone, but one

focused on sorrow and trauma, transforming them into positive energies.

8. Infinite—it's an overall aura booster which increases wellness, vitality, and strength while also having healing attributes.

9. Staurolite—it's a great help for those that want to learn how to channel their energies and emotions.

10. Quartz—it's the overall great for anything gemstone, but its specialty is extreme protection against all types of threats.

While crystals may indeed come as a much-needed helping hand, be aware that every single one has its one unique set of requirements. Some may need to be cleansed (purified by all the energies that they accumulate) on a regular basis while others may need the wearer to undergo a certain set of preparations before actually being "usable." Research extensively before going ahead and buying a random gemstone without knowing what it does and what it needs in order to function properly.

Water Cleansing

In many cultures, water is seen as a connection element between the material and spiritual world. Indigenous communities saw it as the source of all life, and many cultures accept it as a means of cleansing your body and soul. Water heals and purifies, washing off the negative energies. But you don't have to go stand in a waterfall or drip holy water on your head to benefit from its healing qualities. A shower works just as well, as long as you fill it up with your intention of getting cleansed spiritually. It may take some time to master this mental and spiritual exercise, but its effectiveness can't be denied.

Nature, the Ultimate "Grounder"

Spending time in nature benefits anyone, from both a physical and a mental/spiritual point of view. It provides a break from our everyday noise environment, and it brings calmness into the picture. As for empaths, nature can be way more than that. It keeps them balanced and feeling grounded in their own feelings and thoughts. It can also work as a vessel for your negative energy, getting it out of your system and letting it metaphorically "wither and die" in the refreshing scenery. For an enhanced sensorial experience, try walking barefoot through some luscious green grass or letting your feet sink into slightly damp soil.

Alas, there is something that's we're missing. It's great for empaths to go out into the world and use their gift to create a real change for the better, especially if they bring their protection methods along for the ride. Yet, we must not forget one thing: empaths are being with their own dreams and desires. It's way too easy to let that one slip right over your head when you are so focused on the well-being of others. You have your own purpose, besides healing others, and it's ok to hold on to some energy now and then in order to make your dreams come true. It's okay to take time for yourself. It's ok to follow your desires.

Remember that every person, including you, has the right to be happy.

Chapter 8. Simple Everyday Habits to Practice for Feeling Better

In their daily life, empaths are met with a wide array of difficulties, as a result of their way of experiencing their surroundings. We've talked all about cautions and methods that can protect a highly sensitive person's soul from taking on too much of that borrowed external energy. Letting all those aside, I think it's fair to say that we can clearly define a solid number of simple habits that would greatly help an empath go around his merry way in life.

Having a Morning Routine

Most often than not, the way we start our day influences our general mood for the said day and also your energy tone. By having a pre-established routine, you take away some of that stress and anxiety of not having any idea what to do as a new day falls upon you. It also gives you the possibility to plan out your first activities based on what matters the most to you: breakfast, doing some morning exercises or maybe even tucking in some meditation to start the day with a clear mind.

Setting Daily Goals for Yourself

Having goals helps a lot of people feel like they are accomplishing something, therefore finding meaning and purpose for their actions. You can set simple goals to help you surpass some of your anxieties (like slightly extending your socializing time limit for a day or planning a visit in a place that's usually crammed with people) or that will improve your general mood (like fixing a time period of the day in which you are allowing yourself a break, a moment in which you could indulge in your hobbies or otherwise enjoyable activities). As long as you make sure that those goals are achievable, then they can help you evolve and grow as a person without forcing yourself or your limits to the breaking point.

Learning How to Say No

It's understandable that saying no is hard especially for empaths that take it as a personal offense to not be able to please someone's requirements and having to turn them down. But if you care about yourself at least a fraction of how much you do about others, then you must understand that saying no is sometimes necessary. It's a healthy behavior to pick up that will out of emotionally draining situations and stressful scenarios. If you are not comfortable doing something or having a lengthy conversation with someone, saying no it's always the right way to go. Once you've done it a few times, it won't seem that hard anymore.

Maintaining a Healthy Sleeping Schedule

Anyone gets cranky if they did not have their dose of Zs. Sleep is a necessity that we can't deny our bodies, and the recommended eight hours of sleep per night are a *must*, not a *should*. And empaths really need their sleep more than anyone else since it's a way of calming down the nerves and keeping emotional levels in normal parameters.

Play around with Creative Activities

Highly sensitive people have a very strong creative capacity. Picking up hobbies such as writing, painting, crafting or even simply reading can really add up to your spiritual energies. Creative activities help us express ourselves in new and exciting ways, while also offering wonderfully relaxing hours to break out our focus from problems. Books help you explore a new fascinating world full of unique characters and imagery. Your art does not have to be perfect, or even "good" for that matter. Obscure colorful shapes on a piece of paper can make you feel like you've just created the new modern *Starry Night*. Your writing can be just a messy, entangled emotional journal entry. Your crafts might lose a competition against a five-year-old's, but it's a materialization of your imagination, and you'll love it. Maybe you'll even end up finding a lifelong hobby or a hidden talent that you had no idea about.

Get into the Tea Business

And by that, I mean start drinking it! Whatever type and flavor that suit your tastes, though for an empath, the most recommended ones are those with a soothing, calming effect like chamomile or lemon balm. Tea is widely known as the healthiest drink of them all. It has natural antioxidants, it boosts up your immune system, and it can revitalize and energize you without caffeinating your system as coffee does. In fact, completely replacing coffee with tea might be in the interest of an empath. Coffee fills you up with energy, but it also brings the stress and anxiety levels up a notch, and it's not really the type of drink that affects your spiritual energy in the best of ways. Think of it like this: coffee may be the energy drink for your mind, but tea acts as a purifying drink for the soul.

Balance Your Diet and Consider Exercising

This is not about dieting and working out to have the picture-perfect body. Rather than that, the focus should be on having a healthy life. Avoid "bad foods" that are just caloric bombs with no nutritional value (canned food, fast foods, you probably can list many others) and at try to go out for a stroll at least once in a few days. Your mind and soul will thrive in a healthy environment, and this sort of lifestyle will bring you no downsides whatsoever (as long as you don't go overboard with it). If you are not sure what sort of foods are best for you to try getting some advice from a nutritionist. Same goes with exercising—a lot of people have health issues that don't allow them to be as active as others if you fall in this category, consult your doctor, and choose together what's the best way to get some exercise without compromising your health.

Limit Your Social Media Access

As much as social media brings people together, it could also be the source of a lot of unnecessary negativity. On social media, everybody likes to paint the perfect life for themselves, and going to deep in your feed might make you feel like your life is lacking that glam and happiness that others pride themselves with. Don't forget that those picture perfect lives are just that. Pictures. Fabrications. No one has it as easy and good as they'd like, so there's no need to feel that you are inferior in any way for not having what others display in their posts. Besides that, social media can also be a toxic place where people let out the worst in themselves. It's something about the "indirect nature" of online socializing that allows people to be meaner and more critical than in face to face interactions because you can't really see the other person and observe how they are affected by your words. Don't forget that empaths can get their feelings hurt very easily, so it's best to protect yourself from the prying eyes of internet people. Use it with precaution and maybe consider not sharing every little aspect of your life with the whole world.

Surround Yourself with the Right Kind of People

In this situation, it's better to focus on quality than quantity. A small number of real friends make up for a whole army of fake ones that just like to prey on your kindhearted nature. Cherish the people in your life that accept you as you are, with your gifts and your long list of quirks. Consider befriending some other empaths too, since they will understand you the most and you'd both have the opportunity to grow spiritually from this sort of connection. Do not hesitate to cut all ties or limit your interaction with negative influences or people that make you feel uncomfortable. They are not your responsibility. Your well-being should always come first.

Keep Your Environments Tidy

The state of their surroundings highly affects the mood and the spiritual state of an empath. Simply looking at a messy place could bring out feelings of stress and anxiety. Organize your house and workplace to make them relaxing spaces to spend your time in, instead of stressing factors.

Add Some Spice to Your Bathing Time

Bath bombs are all the rage when it comes to turning the simple act of washing into an all-out relaxing experience. You can choose your favorite smells for a special treat or how much *fizz* you'd be comfortable with. Just make sure to carefully check the list of ingredients to make sure that you won't have any unwanted side effects. Also, as a matter of smell, the best options are those with a milder aroma since an empath's senses could be genuinely "bombed" by a strong bath bomb. Go for brands that are deemed safe by the wide public or handmade options to further prevent any sort of unpleasantries.

Get Accustomed to Taking Breaks

Whether it is a nature retreat or a full-fledged vacation, empaths need their rest. They are juggling around not only their emotions but other people's energies too, and that on a daily basis. Their batteries need a frequent recharge to keep the machine "well oiled." There should be no guilt or shame over the fact that you need some time away to unwind and release. Turning this into a habit will greatly increase your life's quality.

There are so many things that empath could take into consideration, in order to not only feel better about themselves but also cope better with their environments. Keep in mind that habits are mostly learned, and you only need an average of sixty-six days to create a whole new one. That does not sound like too much to ask right?

If you feel like some of my suggestions don't suit you in any way, that's completely fine. They're just that: suggestions. You are free to try only the ones that sound good to you. That being said, I really hope that you will really consider the habits that relate to living a healthier life. Our health is one of the most precious things we have, and we should all do our best not to take it for granted and instead maintain it. Your spirit can't grow in an ailing body so make the most out of it and prepare your body for the sort of spiritual evolution that you desire.

Conclusion

Empaths are complex being, and more often than not *complex* is just a nicer way of saying *hard*. It's not just hard to understand how an empath thinks and function. No, the problem is the difficulties that they face in understanding *themselves* and in going through daily life situations.

While we can't argue about the challenges of being a highly sensitive person in today's society, we can't also say that living a healthy happy life is an impossibility for them—far from that. Their gifts allow them such a unique approach to their environments—they can experience a whole new world of energies and feelings that other people are not even aware of. Their emotions are strong, and their kindness is never-ending. They only need to learn how to adjust themselves to protect themselves from all the harmful things that pester our society.

How Can They Adjust?

They can do so by learning how to control their emotions, by being as compassionate toward their own person as they are to others, by accepting their limits and not being afraid to put their well-being first, and last but not least, by growing both as people and as spiritual beings.

That's the purpose of this book: to give empaths a "manual" of what they can do to better themselves while also continuing to lift others up.

If anyone can change for the greater good of the world, then that's the trusty empath—the heart that beats for other before it beats of itself.

Made in the USA
Middletown, DE
17 August 2019